# The Gifted & Talent
# Question & Answer Book
## For Ages 6-8

## By Susan Amerikaner

### Illustrated by Larry Nolte

Lowell House
Juvenile
Los Angeles

CONTEMPORARY BOOKS

Chicago

*To my sister, Ilene, for always being there*
*— S.A.*

Reviewed and endorsed by Q. L. Pearce, author of *The Nature's Footprints* series,
*The Dinosaur Almanac, Giants of the Land, Giants of the Deep,*
and many other books for children.

ISBN: 1-56565-351-3

Publisher: Jack Artenstein
Vice President/General Manager, Juvenile Division: Elizabeth Amos
Director of Publishing Services: Rena Copperman
Editorial Director & Project Editor: Brenda Pope-Ostrow
Managing Editor: Jessica Oifer
Art Director: Lisa-Theresa Lenthall
Designer: Cheryl Carrington
Typesetter: Carolyn Wendt

Lowell House books can be purchased at special discounts
when ordered in bulk for premiums and special sales.
Contact Department JH at the following address:
Lowell House Juvenile
2029 Century Park East, Suite 3290
Los Angeles, CA 90067

Manufactured in the United States of America

10 9 8 7 6 5

# Note to Parents

*Teach a child facts and you give her knowledge. Teach her to think and you give her wisdom.* This is the principle behind the entire series of *Gifted and Talented*® materials. And this is the reason that thinking skills are becoming stressed widely in classrooms throughout the country.

The questions and answers in this **Gifted & Talented**® **Question & Answer Book** have been designed specifically to promote the development of critical and creative thinking skills. Each page features one "topic question" that is answered beneath a corresponding picture. This topic provides the springboard to the following questions on the page.

Each of the six questions focuses on a different higher-level thinking skill. The skills include knowledge and recall, comprehension, deduction, inference, sequencing, prediction, classification, analyzing, problem solving, and creative expansion.

The topic question, answer, and artwork contain the answers or *clues* to the answers for some of the other questions. Certain questions, however, can only be answered by relating the topic to other facts that your child may know. In the back of the book are suggested answers to help you guide your child.

Effective questioning has been used to develop a child's intellectual gifts since the time of Socrates. Certainly, it is the most common teaching technique in classrooms today. But asking questions isn't as easy as it looks! Here are a few tips to keep in mind that will help you and your child use this book more effectively:

★ First of all, let your child flip through the book and select the questions and pictures that interest him or her. This is not a workbook to use one page at a time, building on skills learned as the child goes along. Each page is totally self-contained. Start at the back, the front, the middle — the choice is up to your child!

★ Give your child time to think! Pause at least ten seconds before you offer any more help. You'd be surprised how many parents and teachers give a child little time to think before jumping right in and answering a question themselves.

★ Help your child by restating or rephrasing the question if necessary. But again, make sure you pause and give the child time first. Also, don't ask the same question over and over! Go on to another question, or use hints to prompt your child when necessary.

★ Encourage your child to give more details or expand answers by asking questions such as "What made you say that?" or "Why do you think so?"

The answers in the back of the book are to be used as a guide. Sometimes your child may come up with an answer that is different but still a good answer. Remember, the principle behind all *Gifted and Talented*® materials is to **teach your child to think** — not just to give answers.

This **Gifted and Talented**® **Question & Answer Book** is educational, but your child doesn't have to know that! If the child wants to do only one page, that's great. If he or she only wants to answer some of the questions on a page, save the others for another time. This book will not only teach your child about many things, but it will teach *you* a lot about your child. Make the most of your time together — and have fun!

# Why can't we fall off the Earth?

Everything is held on the Earth by a force called *gravity*. Gravity causes things to fall down toward the center of the Earth. All objects, including planets, stars, and moons, are made up of stuff called *matter*. The more matter something has in it for its size, the stronger its gravity is. Some objects, like the Sun, have lots of matter. The Sun's gravity is much stronger than the Earth's. The Moon's gravity is weaker than the Earth's. You would weigh a lot less on the Moon than you do on Earth!

1. What brings a rocket ship back down to Earth?
2. Why is it so difficult to walk up a very steep hill?
3. Why is it so easy to go downhill?
4. Why is the Sun's gravity stronger than the Earth's gravity?
5. Would things weigh more or less on the Sun than on the Earth?
6. Can smaller objects have strong gravity?

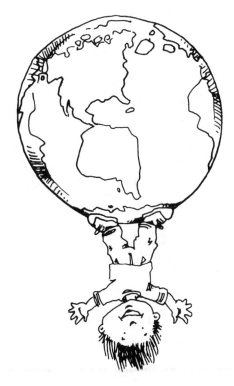

# What makes the seasons?

The Earth is always traveling around the Sun. This path is called an *orbit*. As the Earth travels in orbit, it is also tilted on an angle. Sometimes the part of the Earth we live on is tilted toward the Sun, and sometimes it is tilted away. When the part of the Earth on which we live is tilted toward the Sun, the Sun's rays get to us in a straighter line, and it is summer. At the same time that it is summer for us, another part of the world is tilted away from the Sun — and so it is winter there!

1. When the Earth travels in orbit, does it make a perfectly round circle?
2. What season is it for us when our part of the Earth is tilted **away** from the Sun?
3. How many winter sports can you name?
4. Is every state in the United States cold in the wintertime?
5. If you lived in New Zealand, when would you have your summer vacation?
6. What is your favorite season? Why?

# Do all animals and people sleep at night?

No. Some animals, like the ones in the picture, usually sleep during the day. Animals that sleep during the day — and are up and around at night — are called *nocturnal* animals. Owls, bats, skunks, snakes, opossums, raccoons, frogs, and mice are nocturnal. Sometimes people have jobs that keep them awake at night, and so they sleep during the day.

1.  Why would a desert animal, like a snake, be better off sleeping all day?
2.  Which of the animals above have you ever seen or heard at night?
3.  What do most nocturnal animals do all night?
4.  Can you name some people who stay up all night and sleep during the day?
5.  What would you like about working at night? What wouldn't you like?
6.  If your mom or dad had a night job, how would things be different in your home?

# Do all birds fly?

Not all birds can fly. Ostriches, penguins, and kiwi birds can't fly because their wings are too small to lift them off the ground. Even though they can't fly, they are still birds, because they all have feathers! Kiwi birds sleep during the day and move about at night. They are nocturnal birds.

1. Which bird is **between** the ostrich and the kiwi bird?
2. One of these birds has the same name as a fruit. Which one?
3. Do these birds all live in the same place?
4. Which bird is a good swimmer?
5. Which one is a good runner?
6. What would you do if you found a baby bird that had fallen out of its nest?

# Can flying squirrels really fly?

No, flying squirrels don't fly, they glide. A flying squirrel lives in a hole in a tree during the day and only comes out at night.
At night the squirrels come out and jump onto high branches. Then they leap from the branches, spreading the flaps of skin between their front and back legs. The flaps act like a little parachute that helps the squirrels glide down to the ground.

1. Does a flying squirrel have wings?
2. How do you think a flying squirrel gets back up into its tree?
3. Why is it that you don't see flying squirrels very often?
4. What do flying squirrels like to eat?
5. How can a person do what a flying squirrel can do?
6. If people could fly like birds, what would happen at airports?

# What is a fossil?

**Fossils are the remains of plants and animals that lived a long time ago. Some fossils are the remains of animal bones that have turned into stone. Sometimes the remains dissolve away, but they leave their imprint in the stone — the way you leave your fingerprints on a piece of clay. It may take millions of years for a fossil to form, and so fossils can tell us about animals and plants that lived millions of years ago!**

1. How many fossils in the picture are **animal** fossils?
2. Which is the **plant** fossil?
3. How many leaves are on the plant stem?
4. Which animal could fly? How can you tell?
5. Which animal could swim? How do you know?
6. If you dug up a dinosaur bone in your backyard, what would you do with it? What else might happen?

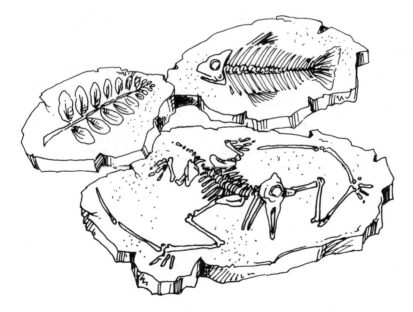

# What is a food chain?

A food chain tells you what eats what! People are at the top of the food chain. For example, grass makes its own food from sunlight, soil, and water. Then cows eat the grass, and they produce milk. And then you drink the milk from cows! There are many different food chains. When you eat hamburger, you are eating meat that comes from a cow. Anytime you eat something, you are part of a food chain.

1. What is at the **bottom** of the food chain in the picture?
2. What other animals eat grass?
3. What is in the **middle** of the food chain in the picture?
4. Do you think that meat-eating dinosaurs were at the top or bottom of the food chain?
5. What other products are made from milk?
6. Can you guess which kinds of fish are at the top of the food chain in the ocean? Why?

# When people get thinner, where does the weight go?

Your body uses food as fuel to keep it going. When you eat more than you need, your body stores the extra fuel as fat. If you eat less food and exercise more, your body needs more fuel and so it will "burn up" the fat. Your body burns fat somewhat like a fireplace burns wood. The fat that is burned leaves your body as fluid when you go to the bathroom and when you sweat. Some of it even leaves your body as tiny particles in your breath!

1. Why does your body build up fat?
2. How is a fireplace a little like your body?
3. Does the fat turn to ashes in your body?
4. Do dogs and cats burn fat like people?
5. What kinds of exercise do you like to do?
6. If you needed to lose weight or gain weight, what would you do?

# What makes plants grow?

**Plants need soil, water, and sunlight to grow. The four main parts of a plant are the flower, the leaves, the stem, and the roots. The green parts of the plant contain *chlorophyll,* a chemical that uses sunlight to make food for the plant. The plant then uses chlorophyll, sunlight, water, and air to make its food.**

1. Which part of the plant "drinks" water?
2. Can plants grow on a cloudy day?
3. In what season do most flowers bloom?
4. If you have a dozen roses, how many roses do you have?
5. Does grass contain chlorophyll? How can you tell?
6. If someone gave you magic plant seeds, what would you grow?

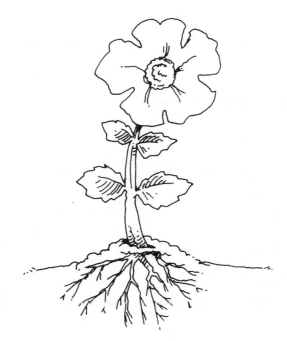

# What can a chameleon do?

A chameleon can change colors to hide from its enemies, or to sneak up on something it would like to eat for dinner. But that's not all that makes it unique. Each of its two eyes can move on its own, so a chameleon can look in two different directions at the same time!

1.  Is a chameleon a lizard, a bird, or a fish?
2.  How does a chameleon hold on to a branch?
3.  What do chameleons like to eat?
4.  What does a chameleon use to catch its dinner? Do you know another animal that catches its food this way?
5.  If a chameleon wanted to sneak up on a grasshopper, what color would it turn?
6.  Would you like to be able to change colors like a chameleon? Why?

# Where does a leopard sleep?

During the day a leopard often sleeps high up in the branches of a tree. Its black spots blend in with the shadowy branches. At night the leopard climbs down to hunt for food. The leopard can see very well in the dark. It moves very quietly on softly padded paws. In this way the leopard can sneak up on other animals, catching them and killing them.

1. Why would the leopard want to stay up in a tree during the day?
2. What word is used to describe animals that are active at night?
3. What does the word **camouflage** mean? What gives the leopard its camouflage?
4. Why do you think a leopard is called a big cat?
5. What other animals are called big cats?
6. If you were writing a story about growing up with wild animals, which animals would you choose?

# Why does milk sometimes smell bad?

If milk sits in your refrigerator too long, *bacteria* — living things that are too tiny for you to see — break down the proteins and fat in the milk. This makes the milk turn bad and smell awful! If you drink the milk before the date that is stamped on the container, it will be fine. But if you wait too long, the slow-acting bacteria start their work!

1. Are bacteria alive or dead?
2. Which of your five senses can you use to tell that milk has turned bad?
3. What could you use to see bacteria?
4. Does all milk come in refrigerated cartons?
5. Do you know what milk contains that is very good for your bones?
6. Pretend that you just won a contest for inventing the world's most unusual milk shake. What did you put in it, and what did you call it?

# Why do we wake up with bad breath?

Tiny living organisms that you can't see — called *microorganisms* — are always inside your mouth. They eat even tinier particles of food, saliva, and dead skin in your mouth. The microorganisms break these things into even smaller bits, and these bits smell bad! When you brush your teeth in the morning, you get rid of all the food for the microorganisms. You also get rid of the food during the day by keeping saliva going as you talk, swallow, and chew.

1. Which part of the word **microorganism** means "very, very small"?
2. What instrument would a scientist use to look at a microorganism?
3. Do you know another word for saliva?
4. If you stayed up all night talking, would your breath smell better?
5. What do you call the tiny wooden sticks used to clean between your teeth? Can you think of another name for them?
6. What happened when you lost your first tooth?

# Why don't these signs have any words?

**The signs below are international signs. They are used not only in the United States, but all over the world. The pictures explain exactly what the signs mean without words, so everyone can understand them. If you were in France and did not know how to read French, you could still read one of these signs!**

1. Which sign would you look for if you were sick or injured?

2. Which sign tells you where to fill up a car with gas?

3. Which sign means "poison"? Does this sign ever mean anything else?

4. What would the sign with the man and the woman on it mean in Japan?

5. What does the "no smoking" sign mean to you?

6. If you could invent a new picture sign, what would it look like, and what would it mean?

# Where does chocolate come from?

Chocolate comes from the cacao fruit of cacao trees, which grow in very hot places. Inside the fruit are cacao beans. When the fruit is ripe, the beans are taken out and left to dry. The beans are put in big sacks and taken to chocolate factories, where they are roasted in big ovens. A machine takes the skins off the beans and grinds and mashes up the beans into a thick, gooey paste called cocoa butter. When milk, butter, and sugar are added to the cocoa butter, it becomes chocolate. Then the chocolate can be made into all kinds of delicious things to eat!

1. Do cacao beans grow **under** the ground or **above** it?
2. Does cocoa always taste sweet?
3. What color do you think cacao beans are?
4. Could cacao trees grow in the United States?
5. Can you think of any other foods that are ground or mashed?
6. If you had twenty-five gallons of chocolate ice cream in your freezer, and the electricity went off, what would you do?

# Does it ever rain in the desert?

It does rain sometimes, but not very much. That's why deserts are so dry. Most deserts are separated from the sea by large mountains. The air that blows from the sea has a lot of moisture, or water, in it. But most of the moisture falls as rain or snow before the winds carry the air over the mountains. The air is very dry by the time it gets to the desert.

1. What is usually **between** the sea and the desert?
2. How can you tell when there is moisture in the air?
3. What kind of prickly plants grow in the desert?
4. What's the difference between the **desert** and **dessert**?
5. Is the air in the picture moving to the **left** or to the **right**?
6. What is a **mirage**? If you were in the desert and saw a mirage, what might it be?

# Why don't people live on the Moon?

There is no air and no water on the Moon. It would be almost impossible to live there unless special places were built in which people could live. Since there is no air around it to protect it from the heat of the Sun, the Moon is boiling hot during the day, but at night it is freezing cold! You would need special gravity boots to help you walk on the Moon, because the Moon's gravity is not as strong as the Earth's.

1. How could you breathe on the Moon?
2. Could plants grow on the Moon? Why or why not?
3. Where could you jump higher, on the Earth or on the Moon?
4. Does the American flag that astronauts left on the Moon wave in the wind?
5. Does the Moon always look the same to someone on the Earth?
6. If you could build a city on the Moon, what would it look like? How would you get water and food?

# How much blood is in a person's body?

Most grown-ups have about seven quarts of blood inside them. This doesn't sound like much, but your blood is made up of lots of things, including about 25 billion tiny blood cells! Blood travels everywhere in your body, and each place it goes it does some work. It takes oxygen and food to the cells that need them, and it carries away waste. Blood also helps your body to fight infections and keeps you warm.

1. What do you have 25 billion of?
2. If you get a scrape or a cut, what happens to the blood after a while?
3. What do you call the tubes that carry blood through your body?
4. Why is it so important to keep a cut clean?
5. How can doctors see blood cells?
6. If you were a doctor, which part of the job would you **not** like? Which part **would** you like?

# Does poison ivy really poison people?

**No. Plants such as poison ivy and oak have oil inside them. If this oil gets on your skin, it can't "poison" you, but it can make your skin break out in an itchy rash. Poison ivy and oak both grow in bushes or vines. They have three leaves on one stem. The best thing to do is to stay away from poison ivy or oak. If you don't touch the leaves, the oil can't get onto your skin or clothes. If you remember this rhyme: "Leaves of three, let them be," you won't get poison ivy or oak!**

1. Which plants in the picture will not make you get an itchy rash?
2. When your skin has a rash, what color does it usually turn?
3. Which flying insect can give you a red, itchy bump?
4. What is the pink liquid that people often use to make their rashes feel better?
5. Can you "catch" a poison ivy rash from someone else?
6. What would happen if poison ivy plants were invisible?

EEK!

# Where does garbage go?

Once the trash collectors pick up the garbage, it is mashed down so that it takes up less space. Trash trucks carry garbage to different places, including *incinerators,* which are like giant ovens that burn up the garbage. Some garbage is dumped into huge trash piles called *landfills.* After the landfills are full of tons and tons of garbage, construction workers cover the landfills and all the trash with dirt. Sometimes buildings are even built on top of landfills!

1. Where is the truck in the picture going to dump the trash?
2. What days of the week do the trash collectors come to your neighborhood?
3. What do you think a **trash compactor** does?
4. How many trash cans does your family leave out for the trash collectors? Are some of them different colors?
5. Do you **recycle** any trash at your home? What happens to the recycled trash?
6. If you accidentally threw the keys to your mom's car in the trash, what would happen?

# Where do things go when they are recycled?

When trash is recycled, it gets used in many ways that help our planet. Soda cans can be melted down and made into new cans, and bottles and other glass containers can be crushed, mixed with tar, and used to make new roads! Old cars are even crushed and melted into steel to make new cars! Trash that used to be food or plants, such as grass clippings or banana peels, gets ground up, mixed with other things, and made into fertilizer to help grow more plants.

1. How many things in the picture could be made from recycled trash?
2. What does fertilizer do?
3. What things did you use today that could be recycled?
4. If more things were recycled, would landfills be bigger or smaller?
5. What things can be made out of recycled paper?
6. How could you recycle some of your old toys and clothes to help other people?

25

# What makes a spider different from an insect?

**Spiders are not insects. They are *arachnids*. Arachnids have only two main body parts, while insects have three main body parts. Most insects also have wings, but spiders don't. Spiders do have a lot of legs, though — eight of them! Insects have six legs.**

1. How many insects are shown above?
2. Which of the insects looked different when it was a baby?
3. If the pictures were in color, what insect would be green?
4. Which insect often gets caught in spiders' webs?
5. What insects like to drink human blood?
6. Little Miss Muffet was **arachnophobic.** What do you think this word means?

# Are bears dangerous?

Giant pandas, and bears that look like toy teddy bears, are dangerous animals! Bears do not see very well and find their food mostly by their keen sense of smell. The smell of food often draws bears close to campsites. Giant pandas eat mainly bamboo and live in China. But, sadly, there are not too many pandas left in the world. American black bears are often found in national parks like Yellowstone and Yosemite. The largest bear of all is the polar bear, which can weigh half a ton and stand ten feet tall!

1. Which bear above is the polar bear? What kind of temperatures do polar bears like best?
2. Is the giant panda **next to** the black bear or the polar bear?
3. Why is it important for people on a camping trip to put all their food and trash away?
4. What do you think the word **keen** means?
5. Do all giant pandas live in China?
6. Why do you think people who lived long ago saw more bears than we do today?

# Who invented electricity?

**No one invented it, but Benjamin Franklin discovered that lightning is caused by a kind of electricity called static electricity. Now people use electricity to create light, heat, and power. Thomas Edison was the first man to figure out how to use electricity for light. Edison invented the lightbulb.**

1. Is the man in the picture Ben Franklin or Thomas Edison?
2. Are either of these men alive today?
3. Do you know what else Ben Franklin is famous for?
4. What is the difference between **inventing** something and **discovering** something?
5. How many things are in the room with you right now that use electricity?
6. What would happen if you had no electricity in your home?

# How does electricity get inside our homes?

**Electrons** are tiny particles that carry an electric charge. The movement of electrons in one direction creates the energy known as *electricity*. Millions of electrons move through cables and wires in the walls and ceilings of your home when you turn on a light switch, a TV, or a lamp. The wires and cables are connected to thousands of other cables that run under and above the ground. They connect neighborhoods and cities to large power plants that send electricity to millions of people!

1. Where are the electric cables in your home?
2. How many things above are powered by electricity?
3. Have you ever lost the electricity in your home? Why?
4. What do you call the place where you plug something electric into the wall?
5. How do scientists see electrons?
6. If you were on a desert island without electricity, what three electric things would you miss the most?

## Do they celebrate the Fourth of July in France?

**No. The Fourth of July is an American holiday. It's the day America celebrates its birthday. A long time ago America was ruled by England, but the people in America wanted to have their own government. On July 4, 1776, the people of America adopted The Declaration of Independence, which said that America was no longer ruled by England. Most of The Declaration of Independence was written by Thomas Jefferson.**

1. Is America more than 100 years old?
2. In what year will America celebrate its 300th birthday?
3. What does it mean to be **independent**?
4. What large body of water is between America and England?
5. What else did Thomas Jefferson do that made him famous?
6. If there had not been a Declaration of Independence, how might things be different in America today?

# Where does plastic come from?

Plastic is a material that can be shaped and molded into many different forms. People make plastics out of different kinds of chemicals. Some of the chemicals used to make plastics come from nature — like rubber from plants and trees — and oil from the earth. People mix these natural chemicals with man-made chemicals to make all kinds of plastics.

1.  How many things in the picture are made from plastic?
2.  Do you know of any things that can be stretched, pushed, or pulled into different shapes?
3.  What does a rubber band do?
4.  How do people get oil?
5.  What else do people use oil for besides making plastic?
6.  Can you make a list of all the things you used today that were made out of plastic?

# What makes a volcano erupt?

Earth is made of many layers of rocks and minerals. Deep inside the Earth it is so hot that the rocks are melted. This hot, melted rock is called *magma*. A volcano is an opening on the surface of the Earth that goes all the way down to where the magma is bubbling. When a volcano erupts, the magma comes out like a river of fire. Once the magma comes out like this, it is called *lava*. Hot ashes, rocks, dust, and gas also shoot up into the air. Lava is so hot (2,000 degrees Fahrenheit!) that it burns everything it touches.

1. Is magma solid or liquid?
2. Why is a volcano dangerous?
3. What does the word **erupt** mean?
4. What makes things melt?
5. What do you think happens to the lava after a long time?
6. How do geologists (scientists who study the Earth and rocks) know when a volcano is going to erupt?

# How does a telephone work?

When you speak into a phone, the vibrations from your voice move through the air into the phone. Inside the phone the vibrations, or sound waves, cause other parts to move back and forth, and the sound waves keep moving and traveling — through the wires and sometimes even through the air — until they reach the person's ear on the other phone. Then the person hears the vibrations as your voice again. This traveling of sound waves happens so fast that you can't even tell!

1. Which phone in the pictures is a **mobile** phone?
2. What does something do when it **vibrates**?
3. Do you know the name of the person who invented the telephone?
4. How is a sound wave like a wave in the ocean? How is it different?
5. Is there sound in space?
6. What is your telephone number?

# Can plants eat bugs?

Some plants can and do eat insects. The pitcher plant has red, sweet nectar inside it. When an insect comes to drink the nectar, it slides inside the pitcher plant and is drowned in the liquid. This nectar is made of strong juices that break the insect down so that the plant can digest it. The pitcher plant grows in tropical countries. The Venus's-flytrap is a bug-eating plant that lives in swamps. When a fly or other small insect sits down on its open leaves, the leaves snap shut, trapping the bug, while juices digest it for the plant. In the wild, some Venus's-flytraps are found only in **North and South Carolina.**

1. Is a pitcher plant named for a water pitcher or a baseball pitcher?
2. How do most other plants get food?
3. Which of the plants in the picture grows in the United States?
4. In what way are these plants like your stomach?
5. Do you know another word for flesh-eating plants or animals?
6. Imagine that you've just discovered a new kind of plant. What does it look like? What will you call it?

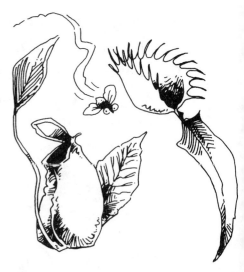

# Which animals make their homes from mud?

Lots of animals, including birds, use bits of mud to build nests. Flamingos use their beaks to scoop up mud and build nests in the water. Swallows fill their beaks with mud from puddles or streams, then they build their entire nests out of mud. Some wasps build nests out of mud, too. Tiny termites use dirt and mud to build homes that are gigantic towers. A termite tower can be taller than a man; even as tall as a two-story building!

1. Who builds the tallest mud home?
2. Can you guess how many termites live inside a termite tower?
3. Have you ever heard of a mud bath? What do you think it is?
4. What farm animal likes to sit in mud?
5. How many insects are in the pictures?
6. Have people ever used mud to build homes?

# Does a firefly have electric sparks in its belly?

No, a firefly's light doesn't come from electricity. Inside the firefly's belly there is a gland called a *lantern.* The light from the lantern comes from a cool chemical inside the firefly's body. Fireflies use their lanterns to flash signals to each other. This is how the males and females find one another.

1. What time of the year do you see fireflies?
2. Why do fireflies flash their lights?
3. Do you know any other names for fireflies?
4. Is a firefly's light hot?
5. What two words make up the firefly's name? Can you think of some more compound words? (Compound words are made by putting two words together to become one word.)
6. Can you make up a story about a firefly that loses its light?

# Why do lightbulbs burn out?

If you look at a lightbulb, you can see a very, very thin wire inside. This thin wire is called a *filament*. When you turn on the light, the electrons flow through the filament, and it gets so hot that it glows. Heat causes tiny cracks in the filament. After a long time, the cracks get bigger until the filament breaks. Once the filament is broken, the electrons can no longer flow through it, and we say that the bulb has "burned out."

1. What makes a lightbulb glow?
2. Why does a lightbulb stop working?
3. Do you know of another kind of bulb that is not a lightbulb?
4. What does it mean when you see a cartoon character with a lightbulb over his or her head?
5. Do you know any words that rhyme with **light**?
6. What would you like to invent that would make your life easier or more fun?

# How did the bicycle get its name?

**The English word bicycle comes from two Latin and Greek words. The Latin word for two is *bi*. The Greek word for wheel is *kylos*. Together these two words form biklos, which means "two wheels." Over many years, biklos changed into the word we know— bicycle.**

1. How many wheels are on a tricycle?
2. What is another name for a bicycle?
3. Why should you wear a helmet when you ride your bicycle?
4. Have you ever seen a unicycle? How many wheels does it have?
5. What else in the picture begins with the Latin *bi?*
6. What do you think the child in the picture is looking at?

# How does a movie move?

A piece of movie film is really one very long strip of individual photographs or drawings. Each single picture is called a *frame*. Most movies contain about twenty-four frames per second. That means your eyes watch twenty-four pictures flash by in only one short second. This is so fast your brain does not have time to tell you that you are looking at different pictures. Instead, it sends the message that you are looking at one moving picture.

1.  What is a single picture on a roll of film called?
2.  What is the name of the machine that shows movies?
3.  Name your favorite movie. Why do you like it?
4.  How fast do you think the pictures in a cartoon flash by?
5.  What things would you need to make a movie?
6.  If you were going to make a movie, what would it be called?

# Who is this man?

This is Abraham Lincoln, the sixteenth President of the United States. People admired him because he told the truth, and they called him "Honest Abe." While he was President, America was fighting the Civil War, which was partly about slavery. Some people wanted to keep slaves, and others didn't. *Slaves* are people who are owned by other people and forced to work for no money. During the time of the Civil War, slaves were often mistreated. Abraham Lincoln believed all people should be free and that no one should be a slave.

1. What was Lincoln's nickname?
2. Do you have a nickname? Do you know anyone who does?
3. Do you understand what it means for a person to be **free**?
4. On what coin does Lincoln's face appear?
5. Why was Lincoln against slavery?
6. If you were President of the United States, what things would you change?

40

# Were pirates real?

Some of the most famous pirates, like **Captain Hook** and **Long John Silver**, were only alive in the pages of books. But there were many other pirates who were real people. Most were criminals who robbed ships at sea. They were cruel and often killed the entire crew after they had robbed a ship. **Blackbeard** was one of the most terrible pirates. There were even a few women pirates! Today, there are still some pirates who attack cargo vessels and steal the products onboard.

1. Who was always chasing Captain Hook?
2. What was the symbol of a pirate ship?
3. What would a big **X** on a pirate map mean?
4. What was pirate money called?
5. What kind of bird did Long John Silver have?
6. If you found a buried box full of money, what would you do?

# What makes a tea kettle whistle?

When the water in a tea kettle is heated, the tiny molecules, or bits, in the water start to move quickly. The hotter the water molecules get, the faster they move, until the water boils. As the water boils, the water starts to become steam. The steam rises and escapes through a hole in the top of the kettle, which makes the whistling noise!

1. If you didn't turn off the tea kettle, what would happen to all the water?
2. Why do you have to be careful when you're pouring water out of a tea kettle?
3. What else can a tea kettle make besides tea?
4. Can you whistle?
5. What people use a whistle to do their jobs?
6. What if you had a magic whistle that only one other person could hear? Who would it be?

# Why does a Mexican jumping bean jump?

**There is a tiny caterpillar, or larva, of a moth inside a Mexican jumping bean. When the caterpillar hatches, its movements cause the bean to "jump"! The caterpillars react to warmth. You can make them jump if you warm the beans by clutching them in your hand.**

1. What makes you come down whenever you jump up?
2. What can kids jump in the playground?
3. What do you call the things that horses jump over?
4. Why is it fun to say rhymes when you're jumping rope?
5. What do you do after you "salute to the captain and bow to the queen ..."?
6. Would it be easier to jump on the Moon? Why?

# Do elephants ever forget?

Yes, they do forget things, but elephants are very smart animals. Some elephants can do all kinds of amazing tricks with their memory, such as learning to remember musical notes. If an elephant becomes close friends with a human trainer, it will remember that person even if the trainer goes away and doesn't come back for thirty years! An elephant remembers things that are important to it, like where to find food. That's a good thing, because an elephant spends sixteen hours a day eating!

1. What part of an elephant's body helps it to remember things?
2. Do you remember your birthday? Why do you think it's easy to remember that day?
3. If an elephant ate hamburgers, how many do you think it could eat?
4. What do you call a group of elephants?
5. Which part of an elephant can act a little like a vacuum cleaner and a lot like a garden hose?
6. Can you finish this story? *Eloise was a little girl who forgot everything. She even forgot her baby brother once! But one day Eloise got a large delivery from her uncle in Africa. It was a baby . . .*

# Can sharks smell things?

Yes, sharks can smell blood up to one mile away! Many animals depend on a keen sense of smell to find food and warn them of danger. When an elephant puts its long nose in the air, it can smell enemies up to three miles away! Turkey vultures flying in the air can smell a dead animal a mile below them. Anteaters use their long snouts to sniff out their food, too.

1. Which animal has the longest nose?
2. What else do you think an elephant can do with its nose besides smell?
3. Can people smell under water?
4. Which animal is called "the swimming nose"?
5. When do people use their noses to warn them of danger?
6. Do certain people and places have smells that you remember? Tell about them.

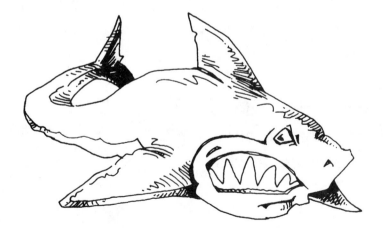

# Who invented the airplane?

Two brothers, Orville and Wilbur Wright, invented the first airplane that had an engine. The first airplane flight, which took place in Kitty Hawk, North Carolina, on December 17, 1903, lasted only 12 seconds! Until that time people had only tried flying gliders. *Gliders* are planes that weigh very little and have no engines. The Wright Brothers were the first to fly a plane with an engine.

1. In what country did the Wright Brothers live?
2. Did the first airplane flight last more than a minute or less than a minute?
3. Which would be heavier, an airplane or a glider?
4. If a glider has no engine, what makes it move in the air?
5. What makes an airplane stay up in the air?
6. If you could invent something new or do something that no one else has ever done, what would it be?

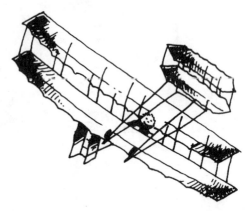

# How does a vacuum cleaner work?

A small fan inside a vacuum cleaner blows the air out of its tank or bag. When the air is blown out, there is a decrease in air pressure, which causes a partial vacuum. A *vacuum* is a space with no air at all. Whenever there is a vacuum, air will try to fill it up again. Air from outside the vacuum cleaner rushes in to fill up any empty space. When the air is sucked in, dust and dirt also get sucked into the vacuum cleaner. The fan blows the air out again, but the dust and dirt get trapped inside the vacuum cleaner bag.

1. How did the vacuum cleaner get its name?
2. What happens when a vacuum cleaner bag gets full?
3. Would a vacuum cleaner work on the Moon?
4. What other kinds of cleaning tools do you see above?
5. If you could invent a new product for cleaning your room, what would it look like?
6. What would it do? What would it be called?

# What makes a stomach growl?

There are fluids inside your stomach called *digestive fluids*. After you chew your food with your teeth, then swallow, the digestive fluids mix with the food. Gas bubbles in your stomach, the food, and the fluids all get mixed and swooshed together, which makes noise! Your stomach growls even more when you are hungry, because when your stomach is empty, there is more air and gas inside it.

1. There is digestive fluid in your mouth, too. What is it called?
2. What do your teeth help you to do besides chew food?
3. How do you think your stomach manages to hold a lot of food at once?
4. Do you know which animal has **two** stomachs?
5. What else can growl besides a stomach?
6. If you could invent a new sandwich made out of all your favorite foods, what would be in it, and what would you call it?

48

# How does a toaster work?

Most toasters work something like a jack-in-the-box! When you put in your toast and set the toaster for how dark or light you want it, you are actually setting a timer. The timer gets wound up inside — just like you wind up a music box or a jack-in-the-box. When the timer finishes unwinding, the time is up and the toast is ready. Then the timer hits a spring that sends the toast up!

1. Which stays in the toaster longer — light toast or dark toast?
2. What kind of energy makes the toaster get hot?
3. What other things have springs?
4. Do you know other meanings for the word **spring**?
5. Why should you never stick a fork, a knife, or anything metal in a toaster?
6. If your toaster was broken, how else could you make toast?

# Can a starfish swim?

No, but it can move. A starfish has tiny tube feet underneath it that help it move very slowly on land and at the bottom of the water. You often see starfish clinging to rocks or even to the pilings of a pier. Starfish usually have five arms. When a starfish loses an arm, it can grow a new one! This ability to grow a new body part is called *regeneration*.

1. Why do you think it's called a starfish?
2. What two words go together to make the word **starfish**?
3. Can you find any other compound words in this book? (Compound words are made by putting two words together to become one word.)
4. Which has more arms, an octopus, or a five-armed starfish?
5. What would you do if you had five or more arms?
6. Can you make up a story about a magical starfish?

# What is the biggest living animal?

The biggest living animal is the blue whale, which can be as big as 90 or more feet long! The blue whale is one of the largest animals that has ever lived — even bigger than most dinosaurs! Whales are among the most intelligent and the oldest of all living creatures. Whales are warm-blooded mammals, but they have no fur. They have a thick layer of fatty blubber under their skin to keep them warm. All whales breathe air, so they have to come up to the surface of the water now and then to get air. Blue whales can live to be 80 years old!

1. If you had a choice, what big animal would you like to be?
2. Why don't whales need fur?
3. What is another word for **fat**?
4. How are people and whales alike?
5. Is a whale a fish?
6. What if you had a friend that was a blue whale? What would its name be? What adventures would you have together?

## Whose picture is on the dollar bill?

**George Washington is on the dollar bill. He led America's soldiers during the Revolutionary War. Later he became the first President of the United States. A well-known folk tale tells of how, when George Washington was a child, his father got angry because someone had cut down a cherry tree in their yard. George supposedly said, "I cannot tell a lie," and admitted that he had cut down the tree.**

1. Do you think it was hard for George Washington to tell the truth about the cherry tree?
2. What does the story of the cherry tree tell us about George Washington?
3. What coin is George Washington's picture on?
4. What is the difference between George Washington's picture on the dollar bill and the one on the coin?
5. How much money is in the pictures below?
6. If you could travel in a magic time machine and meet George Washington, what question would you ask him?

# Who invented cartoons?

No one knows who made the very first animated cartoon, but it was **Walt Disney** who made them famous. In 1928 Disney created the first Mickey Mouse cartoon. Some years later he made the first full-length animated film — *Snow White and the Seven Dwarfs.* An animated movie takes thousands and thousands of drawings to make. When you watch a Disney cartoon, you are really watching thousands of drawings go by — twenty-four drawings every second!

1. If something is **animated,** is it moving or standing still?
2. When the first Mickey Mouse cartoon came out, can you guess who made his high, squeaky voice?
3. How many of the Seven Dwarfs can you name?
4. How is a flip book like a cartoon?
5. Is an **animator** the same as an **illustrator**?
6. If you could create your own cartoon character, would it be a person, an animal, or something else? What would you name it?

# Where does a butterfly go in the rain?

In the rain, butterflies usually rest underneath leaves or stems and blades of grass. Butterflies need sunlight to keep their bodies warm. When there is no sunlight, they fold their wings and rest. Moths are similar to butterflies, but moths are up and about at night instead of during the day. Butterflies and moths usually eat plants and nectar. They live wherever plants grow, except in very, very cold places.

1.  Where do butterflies go at night?
2.  Are there butterflies and moths at the North Pole?
3.  How are moths different from butterflies?
4.  Does a butterfly crawl before it can fly?
5.  How do a butterfly's colors protect it from its enemies?
6.  What is it called when animals disguise themselves by looking like their surroundings? How about people?

# Why do crickets make so much noise?

Male crickets chirp for many different reasons. They chirp as an alarm to warn other crickets of danger. They chirp to attract female crickets. Sometimes crickets chirp when they are fighting. They chirp faster when it is warm outside and slower when it is cold. Male crickets have two 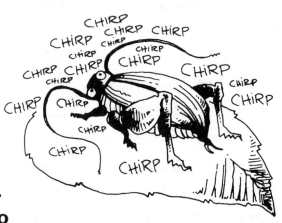 wings that they rub together. This rubbing makes the chirping sound you hear. Female crickets do not chirp.

1. What do you call the sound that crickets make?
2. Why don't female crickets chirp?
3. Would crickets chirp faster in the summer or the fall?
4. Have you ever had a cricket inside your house? What did you do?
5. What do you think crickets eat?
6. Have you ever heard of the book *The Cricket in Times Square*? If you haven't, see if you can find it in the library.

# What was the Pony Express?

In the Old West mail was delivered by Pony Express. A rider would carry a pouch of mail and ride a horse as fast as he could for about ten miles. Then he would switch to a new horse. The rider would keep switching horses until he got where he was going. Pony Express riders were sometimes attacked by Indians, mountain lions, and rattlesnakes. People stopped using the Pony Express when they started using the telegraph to send messages. The messages were electric currents that made clicking sounds. People used a special code to spell words out of the clicks.

1. Why would working for the Pony Express be difficult and dangerous?
2. Why would a rider change horses?
3. Which would be faster, Pony Express or the telegraph?
4. Do you know the name of the telegraph code?
5. What other word that starts with **T** replaced the telegraph?
6. Imagine you are on a stagecoach going to a new town in the Old West. What will the trip be like?

# What is the world's most popular sport?

**Soccer is the world's most popular sport. Every year teams from all around the world try to win the World Cup, the championship game of soccer. When you play soccer, you try to make goals by kicking the ball. Your team gets one point for each goal it makes. You can use your feet or even your head to move the ball, but not your hands! Only the goalies are allowed to use their hands to block the ball. There is one goalie for each team. Soccer is an old sport, even older than football.**

1. What color is a soccer ball?
2. How many players are allowed to use their hands to play soccer?
3. What is missing from the goalpost below?
4. If one team makes five goals and the other makes two, what's the score?
5. Is football more dangerous than soccer? How can you tell?
6. If you were going to be a star athlete, what sport would you play?

# Who invented the umbrella?

**No one knows exactly who invented the umbrella, but we do know that people have been using them for a long, long time. When people first started to use umbrellas in ancient China, Egypt, and Greece, they used them as protection from the hot sun. The word *umbrella* comes from the Latin word *umbra,* which means shade. The first people to use umbrellas in the rain were the Romans. They rubbed oil on their paper umbrellas to waterproof them.**

1. Who first used umbrellas as protection from the rain?
2. Are umbrellas today made out of the same material that the Romans used?
3. When do you use an umbrella to give you shade?
4. What is the name of the story about a nanny who could fly with an umbrella?
5. When is it supposed to be bad luck to open an umbrella?
6. Can you think of three other things — even silly things — that you could do with an umbrella?

# What makes a clock work?

Old-fashioned mechanical clocks and watches run on springs and weights that are inside them. Digital clocks use electricity instead of springs. Inside a digital clock is a quartz crystal. Electricity makes the crystal move very fast — thousands of times a second! Also inside is a *microchip,* which is like a tiny computer. The vibrations of the crystal tell the microchip to change the numbers that you see. The numbers change once every second.

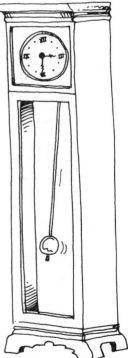

1. Which clock in the pictures is a digital clock? How can you tell?
2. What is the difference between a watch and a clock?
3. You don't plug in a digital watch, so how does it get electricity?
4. What time is it on the clocks in the pictures? Is it morning or afternoon?
5. What time will it be on the clocks in another half an hour?
6. If there were no clocks or watches in the world, how would you know when to get up, when to go to sleep, or when to go to school?

# Answers

## PAGE 5
1. Gravity.
2. Because gravity keeps trying to "pull" us down.
3. Because gravity causes us to move down!
4. Because the Sun is made up of more matter than the Earth.
5. More, because the Sun has more matter and stronger gravity.
6. Yes, sometimes even smaller objects (like some kinds of stars) can be made up of lots and lots of matter squeezed together into a small space.

## PAGE 6
1. No, the orbit kind of makes a flat, round circle called an **ellipse.**
2. Winter.
3. Sample answers: ice skating, skiing, tobogganing, snowboarding, sledding.
4. No, it is usually warm in Florida, Southern California, and Hawaii in the wintertime.
5. In December, January, or February — the winter months in the northern hemisphere, which are the summer months in New Zealand.
6. Answers will vary.

## PAGE 7
1. It is too hot during the day. It is easier to move around at night when it is cooler. It is also easier to find food.
2. Answers will vary.
3. They are usually looking for food.
4. Sample answers: firefighters, security people, doctors, nurses, police officers, bakers.
5-6. Answers will vary.

## PAGE 8
1. The penguin.
2. The kiwi. The bird and the fruit come from the same place — New Zealand.
3. No. The penguin lives in cold places (in the southern hemisphere), the ostrich lives in mostly warmer climates, and the kiwi bird lives only in New Zealand.
4. The penguin.
5. The ostrich.
6. Answers will vary.

## PAGE 9
1. No, it has flaps of skin that act like a parachute.
2. It climbs back up.
3. They usually come out only at night.
4. Nuts and seeds, just like other squirrels.
5. By using a parachute.
6. Answers will vary.

## PAGE 10
1. Two.
2. The one that looks like a plant stem with leaves.
3. Eighteen.
4. The flying reptile. You can tell by the outline of the fossil's wings.
5. You can tell that one fossil is the outline of a fish.
6. Answers will vary.

## PAGE 11
1. Grass.
2. Sample answers: goats, insects, sheep, horses.
3. The cow.
4. The top.
5. Sample answers: cheese, butter, yogurt, ice cream.
6. Big fish, such as sharks. Smaller fish don't usually eat large, healthy adult sharks.

## PAGE 12
1. Because it stores the food as fuel for another time when you might need it.
2. They both burn fuel. A fireplace burns wood; your body burns food and fat. While the fat that is burned leaves your body as water, much of it leaves your body as gas (water and carbon dioxide) when you breathe out.
3. No, it gets broken down into fluid.
4. Yes.
5-6. Answers will vary.

## PAGE 13
1. The roots.
2. Yes, some sunlight comes through the clouds.
3. Spring (unless you live in the southern hemisphere).
4. Twelve.
5. Yes. You can tell by the green color.
6. Answers will vary.

## PAGE 14
1. A lizard.
2. It grips with its feet, like using a pair of pliers.
3. Insects.
4. Its long tongue. Frogs and toads.
5. It would turn the color that would help it to hide the best. If it was in green leaves, it would turn green.
6. Answers will vary.

## PAGE 15
1. It's cool, safe, and a good place to watch out for enemies and food.
2. Nocturnal.
3. To hide; to blend in with the surroundings. Its black spots camouflage it, making the leopard look like part of a tree or bush.
4. It looks like a domestic house cat and is a big member of the cat family.
5. Lions, tigers, cheetahs, jaguars.
6. Answers will vary.

## PAGE 16
1. Alive. Bacteria are one-celled organisms.
2. Smell and/or taste. (But if milk smells bad, don't taste it!)
3. A microscope.
4. No. Some milk comes in powdered form in boxes, and some liquid milk even comes in boxes that do not have to be refrigerated. It can stay unopened in the cupboard for a year. But once you open the box, you must put it in the refrigerator and treat it the same as the other milk you buy.
5. Calcium.
6. Answers will vary.

## PAGE 17
1. Micro.
2. A microscope.
3. Spit.

4. Probably, because that would keep the saliva flowing. (But you'd be very cranky!)
5. Toothpicks. Rest of answer will vary.
6. Answers will vary.

## PAGE 18
1. The sign with the big letter **H** for hospital.
2. The sign with the gasoline pump.
3. The skull and crossbones. It used to fly on flags of pirate ships.
4. The same thing it means here. It shows where a bathroom is.
5-6. Answers will vary.

## PAGE 19
1. Above.
2. No. It isn't sweet until sugar is added.
3. Brown.
4. Hawaii is the only state that is warm enough.
5. Sample answers: peanut butter, corn, wheat, nuts.
6. Answers will vary.

## PAGE 20
1. The mountains.
2. Sample answers: you see clouds; you feel sticky; you feel mist or rain; you see fog.
3. Cactus plants.
4. **Dessert** is something sweet to eat after a meal. You can tell them apart because **dessert** has two **S**'s — because you always want seconds!
5. The right.
6. Something you see that isn't really there. A **mirage** is a "trick" of light caused by the bending of waves of light as they pass through layers of air of different temperatures. Rest of answer will vary.

## PAGE 21
1. Only with a special air tank like the one the astronaut is wearing in the picture.
2. No, because there is no water or air.
3. You can jump six times higher on the Moon, because there is less gravity.
4. No, because there is no air to make wind.
5. No, it goes through four different phases (full, half, crescent, and new).
6. Answers will vary.

## PAGE 22
1. Blood cells.
2. It dries out and clots; forms a crust or scab. Then new skin grows underneath it.
3. Blood vessels. Blood vessels that carry blood away from the heart are called **arteries;** blood vessels that carry blood back to the heart are called **veins.**
4. Germs can enter the bloodstream through the cut and then travel throughout your body.
5. With microscopes.
6. Answers will vary.

## PAGE 23
1. The trees, flowers, and grass.
2. Red.
3. The mosquito, but there are others.
4. Calamine lotion.
5. Yes, if the oil from the person's skin or clothes gets on your skin!
6. Answers will vary.

## PAGE 24
1. A landfill.
2. Answers will vary.
3. It mashes down the trash so it takes up less space.

4. Answers will vary.
5. **Recycling** means reusing objects again (such as cans and bottles), sometimes in a different way. Nature recycles organic trash by itself. It decomposes things like apple cores or banana peels, and the soil uses the nutrients that were inside the food.
6. Answers will vary.

## PAGE 25
1. Lots of things, including the truck, bike, lawn mower, newspaper, fertilizer, plants, grass, and road.
2. It helps plants grow by adding nutrients to the soil.
3. Answers will vary.
4. Smaller.
5. Usually they make more paper goods, such as newspapers, boxes, and cups.
6. Answers will vary, but you could give some things to children in homeless shelters or hospitals.

## PAGE 26
1. Four.
2. A baby butterfly starts life as a caterpillar.
3. The grasshopper.
4. The fly.
5. Mosquitoes.
6. Afraid of spiders (**arachnid**=spider/**phobic**=afraid).

## PAGE 27
1. The one on the far right. Cold!
2. The black bear.
3. So that the bears don't smell the food and come into the campsite.
4. Good, strong.
5. No. Some live in zoos in other parts of the world, even in the United States.
6. Sample answers: Because there were less people, and so there were less houses and roads. There were more forests and more unpolluted rivers and lakes for sources of food for the animals.

## PAGE 28
1. Ben Franklin.
2. No.
3. He helped write The Declaration of Independence. He also invented the Franklin stove, bifocals, and the lightning conductor.
4. When you **invent** something, you make the very first one — it has never existed before. When you **discover** something, you find something that is already there.
5-6. Answers will vary.

## PAGE 29
1. Hidden in the walls and ceilings.
2. The lamps, TV, VCR, radio, and vacuum.
3. Answers will vary.
4. An electrical outlet.
5. With a very powerful electron microscope.
6. Answers will vary.

## PAGE 30
1. Yes, in fact, it's more than 200 years old!
2. 2076.
3. To be on your own; to take care of yourself.
4. The Atlantic Ocean.
5. He was the third president of the United States.
6. Answers will vary.

## PAGE 31
1. The ball, chair, table, doll, bottle, drinking glass, straw, sunglasses, and parts of the bike and the radio.
2. Sample answers: clay, Play-Doh, rubber bands,

Silly Putty, gum.
3. It stretches out and then pulls back. It helps to hold things together, such as stacks of paper or a deck of cards.
4. They drill and dig it out of the earth.
5. Sample answer: gasoline for cars and other engines.
6. Answers will vary.

## PAGE 32
1. Liquid.
2. The hot ash, gas, and lava can destroy plants, buildings, and hurt people.
3. To break out or burst forth, suddenly and often violently, kind of like an explosion.
4. Heat and/or pressure.
5. It cools off and becomes hard rock.
6. Sometimes they don't, but they watch for warning signs such as earthquakes, and steam rising from cracks in the Earth.

## PAGE 33
1. The one that is in the car. It's moving!
2. It moves quickly back and forth.
3. Alexander Graham Bell.
4. They are both waves of energy. Of course, one is in water and one is in air!
5. No, because there is no air through which the sound can travel.
6. Answers will vary.

## PAGE 34
1. It is named for a water pitcher because it is shaped like one!
2. Most plants make their own food from water, sunlight, and air.
3. The Venus's-flytrap.
4. Both have digestive juices that break down food.
5. Carnivorous.
6. Answers will vary.

## PAGE 35
1. Termites.
2. Millions!
3. Believe it or not, some people take baths in special kinds of mud! Mud is good for you and can clean out the pores of your skin.
4. Pigs, but they do not build their homes in mud. They use mud to cool themselves off.
5. Answers will vary.
6. Yes. Adobe houses are made of mud (clay) and straw. People used mud for houses long ago, and they still do in some parts of the world, such as Africa.

## PAGE 36
1. Summertime.
2. The males and females are signaling to each other.
3. Although they are sometimes called glowworms or lightning bugs, fireflies are actually a type of beetle.
4. No, it is cool.
5. **Fire** and **fly.** Sample answers: outside, inside, cheeseburger, football, backyard, homework.
6. Answers will vary.

## PAGE 37
1. The electrons/electricity flowing through the filament make it hot.
2. It stops when the filament breaks.
3. A plant bulb, such as a tulip or a daffodil.
4. It means the character has an idea.
5. Sample answers: night, sight, fight, height, might, kite.
6. Answers will vary.

## PAGE 38
1. Three.
2. Bike.
3. To protect your head and your brain.
4. One.
5. The binoculars for "two eyes."
6. Answers will vary.

## PAGE 39
1. A frame.
2. A projector.
3. Answers will vary.
4. Frames for cartoons go by at twenty-four frames per second.
5. Sample answers: a movie camera, film, and actors.
6. Answers will vary.

## PAGE 40
1. Honest Abe.
2. *Parent:* Answers will vary, but take the opportunity to discuss what a nickname is.
3. Sample answer: not owned or controlled by anyone.
4. A penny. (His picture is also on the $5.00 bill.)
5. Because he believed all people should be free.
6. Answers will vary.

## PAGE 41
1. The crocodile. But also Peter Pan.
2. A flag with a skull and crossbones.
3. That is where the treasure is buried!
4. Doubloons, or pieces of eight.
5. A parrot.
6. Answers will vary.

## PAGE 42
1. It would evaporate as steam.
2. You can get burned by the hot water or steam.
3. Sample answers: coffee, hot cocoa, instant soup.
4. Answers will vary.
5. Sample answers: lifeguard, police officer, referee.
6. Answers will vary.

## PAGE 43
1. Gravity.
2. Sample answer: They jump rope.
3. Jumps or gates.
4. It helps you keep the beat with your feet, like a song.
5. ". . . turn your back to the submarine."
6. Answers will vary.

## PAGE 44
1. Its brain.
2. It's usually easier to remember things that are important to us.
3. A large elephant can eat the equivalent of 2,300!
4. A herd.
5. Its trunk. It can suck in water and then spray it out.
6. Answers will vary.

## PAGE 45
1. The elephant.
2. Grab things; hold things; bring things to its mouth; suck up water and squirt it into its mouth or onto its body.
3. No.
4. The shark.
5. You cannot always depend on your nose to warn you of danger. But you can usually smell smoke, gas, and chemicals, which can all be dangerous.
6. Answers will vary.

3. An airplane.
4. The wind.
5. A pilot flies and steers an airplane, but the engines and wings help to keep it in the air.
6. Answers will vary.

## PAGE 47
1. Because it has a partial vacuum inside of it — and it cleans things!
2. You have to replace it with a new bag.
3. No, because there is no air on the Moon!
4. A mop, a sponge, and a bucket.
5-6. Answers will vary.

## PAGE 48
1. Saliva or spit.
2. Talk.
3. It can stretch and then shrink down again when the food is digested.
4. A cow.
5. Sample answers: lions, tigers, dogs.
6. Answers will vary.

## PAGE 49
1. Dark toast.
2. Electricity.
3. Sample answers: music boxes, wind-up watches, pogo sticks, diving boards, beds, some scales.
4. The season before summer; to leap up; a small flow of water from underground.
5. Because the metal can direct electricity from the toaster into your body and harm you.
6. Over the open flame of a gas stove; in an oven; even on the barbecue grill — all with parental supervision, of course!

## PAGE 50
1. Because it's shaped like a star.
2. **Star** and **fish.**
3. Sample answer: firefly.
4. An octopus, which has eight arms.
5-6. Answers will vary.

## PAGE 51
1. Answers will vary.
2. They have a thick layer of blubber under their skin.
3. Blubber.
4. They are both mammals. They breathe air. People can swim, but they cannot stay under the water for as long as whales can.
5. No, it is a mammal.
6. Answers will vary.

## PAGE 52
1. Yes, because he knew his father would be angry.
2. It tells us he was honest, trustworthy, and brave.
3. The quarter.
4. One is a front view and the other is a side view, called a **profile.**
5. One dollar and twenty-five cents.
6. Answers will vary.

## PAGE 53
1. Moving.
2. Walt Disney.
3. Sleepy, Dopey, Bashful, Doc, Grumpy, Sneezy, Happy.
4. When you flip the still pictures with your thumb, they appear to move, like a cartoon.
5. An **animator** draws pictures for movies or TV; an **illustrator** draws pictures for books or magazines. But they are both artists!
6. Answers will vary.

## PAGE 54
1. To the same places they go when it rains.
2. No, because there aren't any land plants at the North Pole, and it is very, very cold.
3. Moths are active at night; butterflies are active during the day. Some moths are dull and brown colored, while most butterflies are brightly colored. Also, butterflies rest with their wings closed, while moths rest with their wings open.
4. Yes. A butterfly begins life as a caterpillar.
5. Most butterflies look like their surroundings, such as flowers or bushes, so they can hide from their enemies. But some butterflies, like the monarch, stand out on purpose, to warn other animals that they are not good to eat.
6. Camouflage. People use camouflage, too. Soldiers camouflage themselves and their weapons.

## PAGE 55
1. A chirp.
2. Because they don't have the same kind of wings that rub together.
3. The summer, because it is warmer.
4. Answers will vary.
5. Plants.
6. This excellent book was written by George Selden.

## PAGE 56
1. You could be attacked by Indians or wild animals. The weather could be cold, wet, or hot. You'd have to be careful not to run out of food and water.
2. The horse would get tired and slow down, and the rider couldn't wait for the horse to rest. He had to hurry to deliver the mail!
3. The telegraph.
4. Morse code.
5. The telephone.
6. Answers will vary.

## PAGE 57
1. Black and white.
2. Two.
3. The net!
4. 5-2.
5. Yes, it is. Football players use helmets and all kinds of padding. Soccer players only wear knee pads.
6. Answers will vary.

## PAGE 58
1. The Romans.
2. No. Today, umbrellas are made of man-made materials like nylon.
3. Sample answers: at the beach or pool; in the backyard; on a golf course.
4. *Mary Poppins.*
5. You're not supposed to open one indoors.
6. Answers will vary, but perhaps to catch rainwater, to make a birdbath, to sail down a river, and so on.

## PAGE 59
1. The small one without hands.
2. A **watch** is small and portable, and it is usually worn as jewelry: on a strap, a bracelet, a necklace, or hanging on a chain. A **clock** is generally larger and not portable — except for a travel clock!
3. From batteries — batteries make electricity portable.
4. 3:30 in the afternoon.
5. 4:00 in the afternoon.
6. Answers will vary.